ADVENTURERS

SURFING

Jeremy Evans

CRESTWOOD HOUSE

New York

First Crestwood House edition 1993
© Julian Holland Publishing Ltd 1993

First published by Heinemann Library, 1993, an imprint of Heinemann
Educational, a division of Heinemann Publishers (Oxford) Ltd, Halley
Court, Jordan Hill, Oxford OX2 8EJ

Crestwood House
Macmillan Publishing Company
866 Third Avenue
New York, NY 10022

CRESTWOOD HOUSE
First edition

Macmillan Publishing Company is part of the Maxwell Communications Group of Companies.

Designed by Julian Holland Publishing Ltd

Printed in Hong Kong

1 2 3 4 5 6 7 8 9 10

Library of Congress Catalog Card Number 92-43227

ISBN 0-89686-824-9

Acknowledgments
Illustrations: Lawrie Taylor
Photographs: Simon McComb

Thanks to Simon McComb, who took all the photos for this book and
also advised on the contents and technical matters.

Thanks also to Colin Wilson of the British Surfing Association for his
comments on the original manuscript.

Note to the reader
In this book there are some words in the text that are printed in **bold** type.
This shows that the word is listed in the glossary on pages 46–47.
The glossary gives a brief explanation of words that may be new to you.

Contents

What is surfing?

Using the waves

Surfing is about riding waves. Indeed waves are the main ingredient; without them you can't surf at all! The other ingredients are a surfboard, and the few accessories that go with it, such as a wet suit, a necessity if you're surfing in cold water. Full details of these accessories are given further on in this book.

Surfing is fast, sometimes frightening and always exciting, with no noise apart from the hiss of your board and the roar of the waves. There are different forms, including **body surfing** and **body boards**, but this book is primarily about surfing standing up. Riding a surfboard is without a doubt very thrilling; it is also the most difficult type of surfing, necessitating high levels of skill if you are to get past a basic ability level. To become really good requires many hours of practice. And you must be willing (and have the opportunity) to travel all over the world to find the best waves.

Dino Andino rides a mighty wave at Hossegor on the Atlantic coast of France.

Three times women's World Champion Wendy Botha shows her skill surfing a small wave.

Taking a ride

To ride a wave, you must paddle the surfboard to match the wave's speed. It won't pick you up and let you take a ride unless you're in the right place, going at the right speed, at the right time. So paddling the board and controlling it in the waves are among the first things to learn in surfing, before you even attempt to ride.

Once you're up and riding, some of the techniques are similar to using a skateboard. To succeed, you must get a good push-off onto the **wave face** and then combine your balance with the momentum of the board as it heads down the wave face, to execute turns and maneuvers while the wave has the power to carry you.

Surfing potential

Surfing depends on your own skill and the power of the wave. As a sport it is totally nonpolluting and gives a deep insight into the mighty forces of the ocean.

It is a major advantage to try body surfing in the **shore break**, letting the tumbling foam carry you toward the shore. You must be a competent swimmer and feel at ease in big waves. Stamina is much more important than speed or style. Also, you should swim with your head up, so that you can watch out for other things in the water. A surfboard on the loose with its pointed **nose** and sharp-edged **fins** can be dangerous.

5

Origins of surfing

The long Malibu board is still popular with a few surfers today.

How it started

Early pioneers

Surfing is many centuries old. It probably originated in the Polynesian islands of the Pacific. The local fishing people had long known about the power of waves and the behavior of surf, and discovered what fun it was to use a flat wooden board to ride on the waves. In 1777 the British explorer Captain James Cook reported seeing people surfing at Matavi Point on Tahiti and then reported the same phenomenon a year later in the Sandwich Islands, which later became Hawaii. But the Christian missionaries who followed him decided to ban surfing because they thought it was an immoral amusement.

Despite the ban, a few surfers remained in Hawaii, and the sport slowly spread. Prince Kawonanaokoa is said to have surfed in northern California in 1885, to be followed in 1907 by surfing demonstrations by the Irish-Hawaiian George Freeth. Duke Kahanamoku then popularized the sport still further in California, spreading the word as far as Freshwater Beach in Sydney in 1915.

The earliest surfboards were made of solid redwood, were up to 20 feet long and weighed as much as 165 pounds. It wasn't until 1928 that Tom Blake invented a much lighter hollow surfboard in Waikiki and went on to develop the fins.

Surfing comes of age

In the 1940s lightweight boards made from balsa wood revolutionized surfing. These were followed in the 1950s by polyurethane foam and fiberglass boards – still the most widely used materials today. American rock groups led by The Beach Boys told the world about surfing in the 1960s, as did the film *Endless Summer,* which chronicled the adventures of two California boys searching for the "perfect wave."

During the same era, **neoprene wet suits** were invented to allow surfers to stay out in cold water. The short-board revolution began as surfers found that the shorter and smaller the board, the more maneuverable and responsive it would be. New generation surfboards were less than $6^1/_2$ feet long and weighed almost 9 lb. The revolution was helped by the invention of the **surf leash** that connected the surfer to the board. This allowed safer surfing in more dangerous conditions and saved many surfboards from being wrecked on rocky shorelines.

Professional surfing events began in Australia in the 1970s and eventually led to the formation of the **ASP** World Tour. The most recent design breakthrough was the highly responsive **three-fin thruster** design of Australian Simon Anderson in 1981. This design is still favored today in an age when it is the style and commitment of surfers that set them apart from the crowd.

For most surfers today, surfing is about riding a short and very light board.

Types of surfboards

Design

Most surfboards today range in length from around 6 feet up to a maximum of around 10 feet. However, the length of the board is just one of many factors that affect its performance. Most of these are summarized in standard measurements:

● Length from nose to **tail**.
● Width "1 foot off" from the nose and tail (12.2 inches).
● Width at the widest point.
● Maximum thickness, which is measured by calipers.

The first three measurements give a view of the outline of the board, while maximum thickness indicates the **volume** of the board and its distribution, which is important for **flotation**.

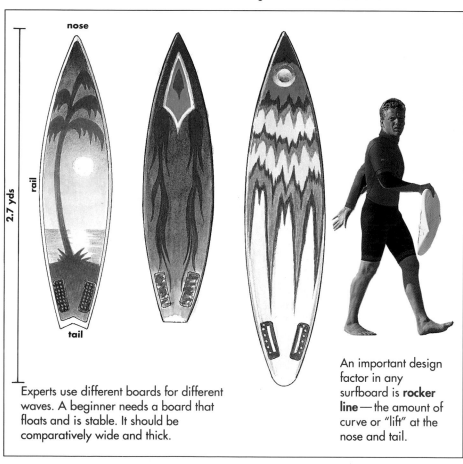

Experts use different boards for different waves. A beginner needs a board that floats and is stable. It should be comparatively wide and thick.

An important design factor in any surfboard is **rocker line** — the amount of curve or "lift" at the nose and tail.

Size

The smaller the wave, the lighter your weight and the better your ability, the smaller the board you can use. In these conditions, very small surfboards are the most maneuverable on the water. However, they are difficult to paddle, and on average or poor waves won't have the volume or sufficient **planing area** to get up and accelerate on the wave face. Wide boards with good volume **plane** earliest and easiest and stay on the plane.

Care and repair

Molded fiberglass boards are relatively durable but are prone to **delamination** with extended use. **Custom boards** require more care:
● Always store a custom board in a light-colored board bag.
● Keep it sheltered from strong sunlight and excessive heat.
● Handle it carefully.
● Cover **dings** (dents or holes) with waterproof tape.
● Repair using suitable custom materials as soon as damage occurs.

Fins

The fin gives the board directional stability and makes it hold in on the wave. Without it the tail would slip away out of control. However, its size must be compromised to allow the board to turn easily as well. Narrow tail boards usually make do with one deep fin; wider-tailed boards have two or three smaller fins called **thrusters**.

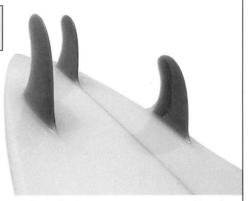

A three-fin thruster arrangement, **offset** for specific conditions.

Custom boards

Custom boards (customs) are hand shaped from a block of polyurethane foam, which is then covered by hand with a fiberglass laminate. The main benefit is that the shaper can make any size, shape or design variation to produce a board that is specifically for you.

The birth of a custom, as the "shaper" gets to work on the foam.

Surfing accessories

Wet suits

The tight-fitting neoprene suit for surfing was developed by Jack O'Neill in the 1950s. It is now considered a necessity for all but the warmest climates. The aim of a wet suit is to keep you as warm and dry as possible. To do this, it must be a perfect fit. It should stretch and move when you do, without restricting you in any way. There should be no loose areas that would allow cold water to collect. The ankles, wrists and neck should keep as much water out as possible so that you get no cold flushes; the zipper should have a watertight flap for the same reason.

The neoprene material can be single-lined, which is usually colored on the inside and plain black on the outside; or double-lined, which is colored on both sides. Single-lined suits are considered slightly warmer, but double-lined suits are more durable. The body of the suit is often thicker than the arms.

This winter suit features double-lined main body areas, with single-lined legs and lower arms for better stretch and ease of movement. Suits like this can be bought in stores or made to measure with your own color choice.

Wet suit care

A good wet suit is expensive, so take care of it. After use, hose it down with fresh water paying particular attention to the zipper. Let it dry, and store it on a thick hanger in a dry place out of direct sunlight. Use warm water and soft soap to clean it.

Leashes

The leash is an elasticized line between surfer and board. It is connected to the tail of the board by a **leash cup/plug**, and to the surfer by a Velcro ankle strap with a swivel fitting. Because the leash prevents the board from getting lost in the surf, the surfer has some help, and the water is safer for others. The drawback is that the surfer may be hit by his or her own board after a **wipeout**.

Hawaiian star Derek Ho with surf leash ready for use.

Cold weather accessories

For cold weather surfing, the **thermal efficiency** of the wet suit can be increased by wearing a neoprene vest or **kidney belt** underneath. Neoprene boots should be soft and close fitting, with an excellent grip on the board. Neoprene gloves, mitts or balaclava are optional.

Protecting the extremities in winter. Mitts are usually warmer than gloves and should be watertight. Wear socks or use talc to help get the boots on and off your feet.

Wax

A good grip on the board is vital. Surfers use special bars of **wax**, which is rubbed onto the deck with long, even strokes. "Soft wax" is for cold weather, while "hard wax" is for hot weather. Always keep a waxed board off the sand. If there's a buildup of wax, use a **wax comb** to cut the surface.

Sunscreens

Unless there is total cloud cover, a good sunscreen is vital. Always wear a nose guard cream in sunlight; protect your whole body if not wearing a wet suit.

11

Where to surf

Finding the right beaches

The first thing to learn about surfing is watching the waves. Watch how they build up and then break when they hit shallow water. Work out their patterns and imagine what it would be like surfing them. Watch the people who are surfing them to gauge the size of the waves and to estimate the power of the **rip current** (rip) flowing back out to sea at the corner of the **break** when each wave has broken. All wave locations are potentially dangerous.

Ideal conditions for getting started are small, clearly defined waves that roll slowly in toward the shore from some way out, breaking on a gently shelving beach. A slight rip will help you paddle back out to the break; a strong rip is a danger for the inexperienced surfer. If possible, keep clear of areas where the break is crowded with other surfers. Such situations can be dangerous and intimidating for the newcomer who lacks sufficient control — you may even injure other surfers. However, never surf alone. Make sure there are people around who know what they are doing and who will keep an eye on you while you are in the water.

Surfers eye up the waves at Perranporth in Cornwall, in southwest England.

The effects of the wind

The best waves often occur when strong winds have passed through, leaving a big **swell** behind. For learning, the ideal conditions are no wind or a gentle offshore wind. This will hold the waves up, produce a good face and allow them to break cleanly. If the wind is blowing onshore from the sea, the waves will break too early and create choppy conditions with a lot of **white water** that cannot be surfed. However, a strong onshore wind can produce its own swell, which can be surfed by those with the ability.

HIGH·SURF AREA

OAHU CIVIL DEFENSE AGENCY

Beginners stay away: experts only!

The effects of the tide

Beach patrol and red/yellow flag.

Waves can be affected greatly by the state of the tide—whether it's high or low, spring or neap. At low tide, small waves can be at their best, while big waves will break hardest because the water is shallower. A beach that shelves very steeply on the shoreline will produce violent, **dumping waves** at high tide that cannot be surfed and are difficult to paddle through. Waves are also affected by the movement of shingle and sandbanks, which are shifted around by wind and tides.

Safety first

● A red flag or disk put up by the lifeguard means DANGER—THE BEACH IS CLOSED to both surfers and swimmers.

● A red/yellow flag or disk means it is a swimming area only—NO SURFING.
● A black/white flag or disk means it is a SURFING AREA ONLY—no swimmers allowed.

Surf breaks

Aerial view of a good left-hander beach break on the Atlantic coast of France.

Beach breaks, reef breaks and point breaks

A break is the place where the waves pitch up to their maximum height, then tumble over and break in shallow water. For surfers it is a general term for where it's all happening. Surf breaks occur when the water depth below the waves becomes less than one-seventh of the distance between the wave crests, and the wave cannot hold its shape any longer. Hence the different "breaks." A **beach break** takes place when the waves break on the sand or shingle of the beach — this break occurs farther out or farther in and has different characteristics depending on the state of the tide. A **sandbank break** takes place when the waves break on a sandbank, close to the beach. A **reef break** occurs where the waves break on a reef offshore, which is formed by a ridge of rock, coral or sand lying close to the surface of the water. A **point break** occurs when the waves wrap around a **promontory** or headland and break on either side. This can sometimes occur together with a nearby reef break.

14

Ground swell

The way waves are formed falls into two categories—**ground swell** and **wind swell**.

Ground swell waves are favored by surfers. They are generated by far-off storms and travel for hundreds or even thousands of miles across the ocean, steadily growing in size. They approach a coastline in long, even and well-spaced parallel lines, until they hit the shallow water and break.

A clean-peeling reef break.

Wind swell

Wind swell waves are windblown waves created by local wind conditions. They are unlikely to get any bigger than 5 feet high and, because they are uneven and more closely spaced than ground swell, tend to break in shallower water close to the beach.

Safety first

● A reef break is dangerous for beginners. It is likely to be fast and aggressive, and rock or coral is hard and dangerous to fall on; in particular, coral causes razor-sharp cuts that may become infected.

A surfer rides a wave near a rocky shoreline—dangerous for the inexperienced.

Wave behavior

How big?

Wave height is proportional to its length. For instance, a wave that is 23 feet long can be no more than 3 feet high. When it exceeds this height because it is being pushed up by shallow water, it will break.

Wave height is measured by doubling the height of the back of the wave to find the height of the face. This measure is an approximation, and surfers usually relate the wave to their own height. Terms used to describe how high waves are include ankle slapper, knee slapper, waist high, shoulder high, head high.

Left or right break?

Surfers always define left and right breaks from their viewpoint looking toward the shore. A **left-breaking wave**, or "left hander," breaks from right to left — from left to right seen from the shore — and the surfer must take off to the left along the wave face to stay clear of the breaking part of the wave. A **right-breaking wave**, or "right hander," breaks from left to right (the surfer takes off to the right). A **closed-out wave** breaks along its entire length and cannot be surfed.

Right break. The surfer goes right, ahead of the surf where the face is steepest.

Rip dangers

A rip is a surface current between breaks, where the water that comes in with the waves flows back out to sea. Experienced surfers will often use slow-moving rips to paddle out to the break. Fast-moving rips are potentially very dangerous as they are impossible to paddle against. If you are caught in a rip with or without your board, the normal self-rescue technique is to allow the rip to carry you to deeper water, where it becomes less powerful, and then swim across to the nearest break, which will wash you back to the shore.

Undertow

If closely spaced, incoming waves prevent the water landing on the beach from returning to the sea via rip currents, there will be an outgoing undercurrent running seaward beneath the incoming surface water. This is known as the **undertow** and is particularly powerful on a steeply shelving, dumping beach.

Stretch before you surf.
Above: On the beach in France. Always warm up and stretch before you go out in the surf. Left: Top pro surfer Barton Lynch prepares himself for the Hot Tuna finals in Newquay.

Avoiding collisions

Rights of way

Horrific accidents can be caused by high-speed surfers, and with good waves crowded with surfers, it is important to understand the rules of surfing.

When a surfer is riding a wave, he or she has undisputed right of way, and all other surfers have to keep clear. This is equally true of surfers who are paddling back out. They must keep clear of the unbroken face of a wave being ridden by a surfer.

If two surfers start paddling for the same wave, the surfer on the inside who is closest to the curl (the steepest part where the wave is starting to curve over and break) has right of way. However, if it is possible to ride the wave both right and left, you could share the wave if you don't interfere on **takeoff**.

Newcomers to surfing must respect those with greater experience, and also respect locals who will not welcome pushy outsiders. There are never enough good waves, and the best surfers who have had years of practice will always get the best waves. However, a good wave cannot be ridden well by an inexperienced surfer, so it is better to give way and learn to ride all waves, good or bad.

Windsurfer meets surfer on a wave at Hookipa. The surfer always has right of way.

Wipeouts

Falling off your board and wiping out can be dangerous, especially in big surf. Always try to fall away from the wave's breaking lip, where you risk collision with your own surfboard. Think what's under you as you fall. If it is soft sand, that's OK; if it is rock or coral, try to land feet first and roll into a ball, protecting your head with your arms, allowing the wave to roll you in. The main thing is to relax. Take a deep breath and dive to get beneath the main area of turbulence. Open your eyes underwater to look for a patch of still water to break surface. Then be prepared to take a deep breath and dive again to get under the following wave.

A surfer wipes out on Oahu, Hawaii.

Safety first

● Learn and abide by the rules of surfing.
● If you wipe out, fall away from the **impact zone** where the falling lip will hit the water ahead.
● Don't surf near rocks unless you know the break well.
● Don't go in the water too soon after eating. If you experience cramps, get out of the water.
● Always stretch and exercise before you surf.

Dropping in at Hossegor. Don't do it!

19

Dry-land practice

How to stand

Before taking to the water you should practice a takeoff on dry land. Lay the board down on a flat surface, removing the fin if necessary. Lie flat along it, with your toes right on the tail, and grip the **rails**. In one movement push up with your arms and slide your feet up under your body to get into a crouching position. Slide your hands back and sit back on your feet, and then stand. You should aim to do all these things from lying to standing in one fluid movement.

2 From flat on the board push your body upward.

1 Lie on the board with your hands on the rails.

3 Bring your feet beneath you and then sit back.

4 Stand up quickly — note the surfing body position.

Foot and body position

Surfers always stand with the same foot forward. This is important, as the surf leash is attached to the back foot. If you attach it to the front foot, you will get tangled and wipe out. **Regular stance** or "natural" is left foot forward. **Goofy stance** is right foot forward.

If you stand too far back, the tail will sink; if you stand too far forward, the nose will dive. Both feet should be across the central stringer at right angles to it, with legs bent, body crouched and feet about shoulder width apart.

A relaxed stance with arms used to balance.

Knees and ankles are flexed as the surfer goes with the wave and the board.

Getting out

Paddling

Practice paddling on flat water. You must lie on the board so that it is balanced with the nose lifted just above the water. If you lie too far back, the tail will sink, and it will become difficult to drive the board forward. Both legs should be tight together, with nothing dragging in the water to slow you down. Your chest and shoulders should be raised with head upward to allow easier breathing, as you paddle with your arms in a crawl action. Practice paddling hard in short bursts, as you would to catch a wave. Also practice turning, by shifting your weight back and kicking your feet while your hands act like rudders.

Paddling — note how the upper body is raised.

Leaving the water's edge

Carry the board down to the water's edge. If the board is too wide to carry side-on under your arm, carry it flat on your head. As you walk into the water, hold the board ahead of you, to one side. Make sure you're in deep enough to clear the fins, and as a wave comes toward you, push the board forward, throw yourself on and start paddling immediately.

Getting through waves

The rip allows surfers to paddle out around the side of the **breaking** or **broken waves**, but they always have to be faced up to sometime. If you see a wall of white water heading toward you, the easiest but least effective method is to slip to the back of the board, turn it around to face the beach, sit astride it and let the wave wash over you with your feet dragging so you don't get washed all the way back in.

You can sometimes deal with a small broken wave by simply lifting your body off the board and letting the white water pass under your body. A more effective method is to try to get through by sinking the nose, either by moving forward on the board or getting off and holding the nose down.

Safety first

● Never paddle out if conditions look dangerous.
● Be aware of other people in the water. Never throw away your board without a leash. It could hit someone and cause serious injury.
● If you dive down to avoid a breaking wave, watch that your own surfboard doesn't collide with you on the surface.
● Keep clear of the impact zone, where the lip of the wave lands.

Lost board in the impact zone. Either hang back or paddle hard to avoid it.

Wave choice

The right wave

Having watched the waves from the beach, you can now choose your wave from the water. Remember that it may have traveled many hundreds of miles and is now about to peak and break just for you. Choosing and catching the right wave is an art, and perfect timing is essential. If you catch it too soon, the wave will pass under your board and carry on without you; if you catch it too late when it is too steep, you may get pitched head over heels. Before attempting to ride unbroken faces, learn to catch a wave and stand up in the **soup**.

This clean, left-breaking wave makes a perfect choice.

Wave facts

Wave speed is the speed at which a wave travels in open water — up to about 35mph — before slowing in shallow water. Wave length is the distance between two wave crests measured in seconds. Wave shock is the force of the waves as they hit a land mass. Wave train is a succession of similar waves at equal intervals. Wave peak is the highest point of the wave where it will start to break, the perfect place for takeoff. Wave threshold is the personal limit to the size of a wave that a surfer will attempt to ride.

The lip of the wave pitches over and breaks next to the steepest section.

Closed-out waves

Closed-out or **sneaker waves** are for experts to ride only, but are sometimes unavoidable when paddling out to the lineup where the action takes place. If you are confronted with one when paddling, the only way to get through may be to sink the board or roll under it. Alternatively, turn the board and ride in with it.

Riding a closed-out wave at Maalaea on Maui.

Taking off

Catching a wave

When you have paddled out through the breaking waves, sit up and turn the board around. There is usually more than one wave in a set. Be prepared to wait for the best-shaped wave of the set. Check that there is nothing to collide with ahead, and then paddle toward the shore, keeping ahead of the wave and watching behind. Your paddling speed must match the wave's speed, so paddle like mad or it will pass under you. Then give a final stroke as the board heads down the wave face. The first few times, lie down and surf the wave to the shore. When you're confident about catching it, go to the standing position.

Shark's-eye view at Lobos Island!

The moment of takeoff on the critical steep section of a wave. The surfer paddles furiously to match his or her speed to the wave's. As the board is picked up, the transition from paddling to standing and riding is made in one swift action.

For the first attempts, the surfer rides the board straight in to the shore.

Forehand and backhand takeoffs

Once you have mastered taking off straight down a wave face, the next steps are **forehand** (or **frontside**) and **backhand** (or **backside**) takeoffs, which lead to riding along the wave face for a longer time. In a forehand takeoff you are starting off at an angle, in the same direction the wave is going to break, prior to riding front side to the wave face. A backhand takeoff is the more difficult option. In this maneuver you can't see the wave behind when you are taking off at a tighter angle before riding back side.

Safety first

● If you lose your board, grab the leash as close to the board as possible to retain control.
● If you are on collision course with another surfer, sink the tail of your board to slow down and steer in toward the beach with the wave.

Surfing moves

Bottom turns

The **bottom turn** is the first turning maneuver. It follows the takeoff and the drop down the wave face and is executed at the bottom or out in front of the wave, to bring the rider back up onto the face. The bottom turn is executed by bending the knees as low as you can, and then rising up and leaning the board in the direction you want it to go, with momentum carrying you through. If instead you want to get out of the wave, the method used is the kick out. This is done by leaning back, lifting the nose and turning the board where you want it to go.

A fast, forehand bottom turn, which is executed well below the crest of the wave.

Forehand and backhand bottom turns

Druston Ward executes a backhand bottom turn at St. Agnes in Cornwall.

For the bottom turn the surfer rides down the wave face, always looking in the intended direction of travel as these photos show. Hitting maximum speed at the bottom of the wave, he or she flexes the knees and leans over to weight the inner rail and tail of the board, using his or her front foot to guide it back up the face ready for the next change in direction. On the way up the face he or she will then level the board out and decide whether to head for the lip or ride the unbroken face. The forehand bottom turn — which is executed riding front side to the wave — is the easier maneuver as it gives a better view of the wave. During the backhand bottom turn the surfer has a very restricted view of what is happening because the critical section of the wave is crumbling behind him or her. This is demonstrated by the photo of surfer Druston Ward.

Advanced surfing

Cutbacks

The **cutback** is one of a coordinated series of turns on the wave. These turns are achieved by split-second **weighting** and unweighting of the board for fast, controlled changes in direction, using short multifin boards that are designed to be kept turning from rail to rail, even though they may be comparatively slow in a straight line. The amount of rail used governs the speed and the arc of the turn. Too much rail and too tight a turn, and you risk stalling the board.

The cutback is an S-shaped maneuver that brings the surfer back to the breaking section of the wave. He or she then turns sharply again along the wave face, by snapping the board around. In competition surfing it is a complete change of direction of at least 120 degrees. Here Fabio Gouveia performs the more difficult backside cutback at Hossegor in France.

Top turns, off the lip and off the top

The **top turn** is a slowing-down maneuver at the top of the wave, to change direction for a better ride back down the wave. Other variations include the **off the lip**, performed by cutting steeply up the wave face to a near vertical stall on the lip, and then instantaneously turning the board back down the wave face. The similar **off the top** consists of smashing the board off the top of the lip. There are a number of "off the..." expressions — **off the face** means any turn on the face.

Safety first

● Drowning is always a possibility when surfing, and any surfer should study the basics of first aid with particular emphasis on **artificial respiration**. The technique must be taught by a professional, even though it is relatively simple. The aim is to get air into the victim's lungs as fast as possible. This should be performed in the water if necessary, having first removed any obstructions from the casualty's mouth.

An "off the top" uses the full power of the wave to ride back down the fall line.

Roller coasters

The **roller coaster** is a climb up and drop down maneuver on the face of a wave. The surfer comes out of a very fast bottom turn, slides the board up the wave face and then rebounds off the lip at the top of the wave. It can be used to get straight over the top of ridable sections of broken white water on the way back to the clean wave face, rather than going below the white water. This is called a floater. One of the skills in the roller coaster and other advanced maneuvers lies in keeping the board moving. Experts pump their board by rocking it from rail to rail, to push air underneath and keep the board planing over the water.

Safety first

Surfers spend a lot of time in the water, and in some parts of the world there is a remote chance of shark attack. Only a few of the many shark species are known to be dangerous, and of the 100 or so shark attacks reported annually on all water users, only about 30 per cent are fatal. If you fear a shark attack:
● Don't surf alone.
● Don't surf at night.
● Get out of the water if you're bleeding — sharks have a great sense of smell.

Roller coaster — Druston Ward takes a shortcut over the white water, riding back side.

Reentries

The **reentry** is an extreme version of the roller coaster. The surfer drives his or her board to the very top of the wave, momentarily skates along the top of the lip, keeping just ahead of the critical breaking section and then drops back down the face. The most difficult type of reentry is to go past vertical on the way up, or to recross the path of the vertical ride on the way down. This maneuver requires perfect timing and balance as the surfer hits the lip, almost instantly changing direction to head back down with it. If the surfer hits the lip too late, he or she will be engulfed in the white water.

Druston Ward performs a radical reentry, back side to the wave. He drives his board up the face to meet the curling lip, skates his board along the top of the wave, and then redirects it down the breaking face in a dynamic maneuver. Note how he crouches and steadies himself while riding down the foam; some surfers may grab the inside rail.

Survival duck dives

All advanced surfers must be familiar with the duck dive, which is the most practical method of getting through white water by diving the board under the wave. While lying flat on the board, paddling toward the white water, push up on your arms and then push the nose down under the broken wave as it engulfs you. Follow this movement through by kicking your legs to submerge the board as deeply as possible. Then push your foot against the tail to make the nose of the board head up toward the surface, with a good kick from the other leg to get you going in the right direction.

A lone surfer about to duck dive through a closed-out set of white water — the only way to get through to the other side.

Roundhouse cutbacks

This is a cutback during which the surfer keeps up speed and momentum to avoid stalling, while going through a large turn of up to 180 degrees or more. Note the wake of the surfer showing the full arc of the turn.

Surf reports

Most major surfing areas have regular **surf reports** broadcast by local radio stations, published in local newspapers and available on phone-in services. The surf report should also be posted by lifeguard stations. The information given is similar to the weather forecast, but is tailored to surfers' specific requirements. The things surfers want to know include the height of the swell, the swell direction and the wave shape, which is described as clean, good, fair or poor. It may also be important to know air temperature, water temperature, the wind speed and the times of high and low tide.

Floaters

The floater lets a surfer ride the board horizontally across the white water after the wave breaks. It relates closely to a reentry without direction, when the wave is about to close out. A floater reentry is another name for a roller coaster. The board moves relatively slowly across the white water and becomes difficult to stand on, and timing is essential. Here a couple of surfers show how to float across that white water.

Tail slides

Todd Holland cuts back front side at Hossegor, and then he tail slides his board through the white water of the breaking lip. The **tail slide** is a variation on the floater. In this action the surfer lets the board drop tail first down the breaking wave while keeping control of the board's direction.

"Kneelos"

Kneeboarders or **"kneelos"** ride on their knees on specially designed boards. The main advantage is that they can maneuver in tight spots where a standing surfer would lose control. At around 62 inches kneeboards are usually shorter than normal surfboards, but they need to be wider to be stable enough to paddle. Most kneeboarders wear flippers to help with paddling and takeoff, and thick kneepads are essential.

Aerials

An **aerial** is any maneuver in which the surfer and surfboard get completely airborne off the wave, and then reenter the face or lip and continue riding.

A basic aerial is the **ollie-pop**. The surfer uses the cross current across the wave as a launch pad, lifting his or her feet to allow the board to get airborne. Landing is achieved by flexing the knees and ankles to absorb the impact and prevent the board from diving under.

An off-the-lip aerial is more critical, hitting the lip to send the board into vertical takeoff. The surfer keeps low as he or she hits the lip, grabbing the outside rail. As the board takes off, the surfer stands upright while keeping the board in a horizontal position.

A backside aerial at Rocky Point, on Oahu, Hawaii.

Body boards

Body boards are often called boogie boards and have been developed from the invention of a solid, soft foam plastic board by Californian Tom Morey in the early 1970s. These are small, wide boards on which the surfer lies, usually around 3 feet long by about 18 inches wide. Essential accessories are a pair of swim fins, used to drive the board and help it through maneuvers.

The main attraction of the body board is that it is very easy to ride, and fairly easy to perform quite difficult maneuvers. An additional advantage is that its light weight and soft construction make it safe in the surf, though the more rigid the board, the better it will perform.

Tube rides

Nothing in surfing is as emotive as tube riding. The **tube** is the tubular shape of a perfect breaking wave, when the plunging lip throws itself out in front of the advancing face. A ride through a tubing wave that completely encloses a surfer is the highest scoring ride in a surf contest, with the degree of difficulty measured by the size and hollowness of the wave and by the length of time in the tube. During a tube ride the surfer will completely disappear behind the curtain of the breaking wave and then hope to emerge unscathed at the other end before the wave collapses.

Wave skis

The **wave ski** rider sits on the board, is held in place by a seat belt and uses a twin-blade paddle to drive the wave ski and help it change direction. Skis range in length from around 72 inches to over 3.3 yards, with the shorter skis offering the best performance to more experienced surfers. The best wave skis are hand shaped and custom built for top riders.

Marty Thomas goes for maximum points during the Rip Curl Pro event at Hossegor.

He rides frontside along the face as the tubing lip curls over and covers him.

Marty finishes his ride, timed to perfection, as the lip collapses and crashes.

International competition

THE ASP

The Association of Surfing Professionals (ASP) runs an annual circuit of World Tour events for the small band of 44 top men and 24 top women who rank as the best competition surfers in the world. The ASP is a nonprofit-making organization dedicated to the promotion and excellence of surfing events worldwide, operating from dual offices in Sydney, Australia, and Huntington Beach, California. In 1992 the ASP introduced a two-tier system of events, running both the World Championship Tour and the World Qualifying Series.

The WCT Tour of 1992 consisted of 12 men's contests, 16 women's contests and a long-board World Championship. These events took place between April and December. Surfers visited big-wave locations in Australia, South Africa and Reunion Island in the spring; they crossed the Atlantic to Europe for three events in France and one in Spain on the Atlantic coast; and then they returned to the other side of the world for the final events of the year in Japan, Brazil and Hawaii. The World Surfing Championships are held every two years.

Tony Ray in action near the critical section at the 1991 Rip Curl Pro at Hossegor.

The scoreboard at the Hot Tuna Surf Masters event at Newquay, Cornwall.

THE WQS CIRCUIT

The World Qualifying Series is a feeder system for the World Championship Tour, based on over 50 events worldwide including domestic circuits such as the US Pro Tour, the ASP Australia Series and the South African Surfing Series. The top 28 men on the WQS circuit gain automatic entry in the WCT for the following year, together with the top 16 men and top 16 women from the previous year's WCT.

CONTEST FORMAT

The basic surf contest format is one-on-one, with two surfers out on the water together for a fixed period of about 20 minutes. During that time five judges on the beach will score their performance on a maximum of ten waves. The scores from the best four waves for both surfers are then added together to find the winner, who goes through to the next heat, eventually reaching quarterfinals, semifinals and finals. Due to pressure of time, an alternative system can be used, with four surfers in each heat and the top scoring two going forward to the next heat.

Judging is not without its problems and is always open to disagreement. It becomes a serious affair when large amounts of prize money are offered, as at ASP events. In the early days of competitive surfing, the surfers on the beach would simply vote the winner. However, today more sophisticated judging methods are used in surfing competitions with precise scores on every aspect of wave riding and allowances for changes in wave conditions that might favor some surfers.

The big stars

Martin Potter, the 1989 World Champion, in action at Biarritz.

Competition success

● Study and remember the competition rules.
● Watch the surf before you go out, to decide where you will be riding and see what you can do with the waves.
● Use a watch. Contest heats are run on a time system.
● Having the right board for the conditions is important when all the surfers are closely matched.
● Don't stand up on the board until the wave is worth riding. You are marked from that moment.
● If possible, go for the biggest waves, which allow you more space for better maneuvers. If you see a great wave coming up, be prepared to change waves.
● Respect the rights of the other surfers in the competition when on the waves.

Wendy Botha — former World Champion.

Top men and women

The top ASP (Association of Surfing Professionals) members have a rich lifestyle as they surf the greatest breaks in the world. They can also earn a high income with the prizes for the ASP World Tour in excess of $1 million and additional major earnings from their sponsors.

There have been many legends in the world of surfing since Peter Townend (Australia) won the first ASP World Championship in 1976. Tom Curren (USA) has been described as "the most extraordinary competition surfer in history." World Champion in 1985, 1986 and 1990, he surfs daily at his adopted home on the Basque coast of France. Australia's answer is said to be Tom Carroll, rated the best in Hawaii and World Champion in 1983 and 1984 when he took over from fellow Australian Mark

Richards; four times World Champion 1979–1982. In 1989, Martin Potter became the only Briton to ever win the World Championship, though for many years he has lived in Australia and South Africa. Americans and Australians have continued to dominate, with Barton Lynch (Aus) winning in 1988 and Damien Hardman (Aus) winning the World Championship in 1987 and 1991.

On the women's side, Wendy Botha from Australia won the World Championship three times, in 1987, 1989 and 1991, while Pam Burridge (also from Australia) won in 1990. Kim Mearig from the USA won in 1983; Frieda Zamba (also from the USA) was World Champion in 1984, 1985, 1986 and 1988. Frieda retired after her fourth world title.

Kelly Slater, an explosive surfer from Florida, free surfing in France.

A world of surfing

When the surfing bug bites, surfers travel the world searching for the ultimate wave. They're looking for perfect ground swell waves, traveling in well-spaced, well-behaved sets, with beautiful clean faces that just go on forever. They're also looking for a surf spot where the air is warm, the water is warm, the locals are friendly and there are no crowds on the waves.

EUROPE

Surfing in Europe is dependant on Atlantic weather systems, with the southwest corner of France rated as the best area in late summer through to autumn. Biarritz, Hossegor and Lacanau are among the well-known and very popular wave spots, while other lesser known breaks can be found at Guethary and Henday. River-mouth breaks are in abundance down the adjoining Spanish coast, and extend into Portugal as far down as Lisbon, where a left-hand break works at Estoril.

Further north, Britain's surf breaks were rated good enough to stage an ASP contest at Newquay on the north coast of Cornwall, and the surf breaks of Devon and Cornwall are usually rated as the best in Britain with consistent swell conditions in all but the summer months. There are also good beach breaks in many spots around the UK coastline. Notable locations include the Gower Peninsula and Freshwater in Wales, and for those who live in the very far north the potential stretches as far as Thurso on the north coast of Scotland.

Heavy soup at Fistral Beach, Newquay, during the Hot Tuna Surf Masters.

Ala Moana on the island of Oahu, Hawaii, one of the great surfing spots.

THE UNITED STATES AND AUSTRALIA

Modern surfing began in California, and this is where Americans find the best waves. The most famous Los Angeles break is Malibu, which is blessed with south swells in the summer and north swells in winter. To the north are Secos, Country Line and Rincon, with Hammonds Reef, Gaviota and the Ranch farther up the coast offering a wide choice of good breaks for the experienced surfer. Beach breaks in the southern part of the state include Newport Beach, Cottons Point and Trestles, while further afield the East Coast and Gulf Coast make the most of local wind-blown waves.

Australia has numerous great surf breaks. Among the most famous are Byron Bay on the most easterly point of Australia, and nearby Lennox Head. Other well-known spots include Noosa Heads at the top of the east coast, the Gold Coast, and Narrabeen and Cronulla among the breaks near Sydney. There are good surfing conditions along the south coast as far as Margaret River near Perth in Western Australia, with many uncharted breaks beyond.

FURTHER AFIELD

Australian surfers head for Bali, reckoned to be a surf paradise from March to September, and many get as far as Mauritius with its Indian Ocean swells. Americans favor the Baja Peninsula close to home in Mexico, or better still head for Hawaii, which from November to March is reckoned to have the best surf in the world. The islands of Maui and Oahu are most favored, with Oahu's north shore rated the prime surf spot in the world.

South Africa has its own excellent surf locations, while in North Africa, surfers escaping the European winter find spots on the Atlantic shoreline of Morocco. Further offshore, the Canary Islands of Fuerteventura and Lanzarote get the best winter storm Atlantic swells and have their own surfing communities.

45

International associations

Association of Surfing
Professionals
P.O. Box 309
Huntington Beach, California 92648

Australian Surfriding Association
P.O. Box 230
Torquay 3228
Victoria

British Surfing Association
Champions Yard
Penzance
Cornwall
TR18 2SS

French Surf Federation
BP-28 Plage Nord
40150 Hossegor
France

Hawaiian Surfing Association
P.O. Box 1707
Pearl City, Hawaii 96782

New Zealand Surfriders
Association
PO Box 1026
Gisborne

Professional Surfing Association of
America
530 6th St
Hermosa Beach
California 90254

United States Surfing Federation
11 Adams Point Road
Barrington
Rhode Island 02806

Glossary

aerial: a maneuver where the board leaves the water
artificial respiration: forcing air into the lungs
ASP: Association of Surfing Professionals
backhand/backside: surfing with your back to the wave
beach break: waves breaking on a beach
body boards (boogie boards): small surfboards that you lie or kneel on
body surfing: surfing without a board
bottom turn: turning at the bottom of the wave
break: where the waves start to break
breaking/broken wave: when the wave crumbles and turns to white water

closed-out wave: a wave that breaks along its full length
custom boards: handmade boards
cutback: a move from the top of the wave
delamination: when fiberglass comes away from the foam core
dings: dents, holes or cracks in a surfboard
dropping in: entering someone else's wave
dumping waves: waves which break on a steep shoreline
fin: an aerofoil which controls the direction of the surfboard; also called a skeg
flotation: the amount of weight a surfboard will carry when paddled,

determined by its volume

forehand/frontside: surfing with your front to the wave

goofy stance: standing with your right foot forward on the board

ground swell: waves which have traveled across the ocean

impact zone: the point where the breaking wave crashes down

kidney belt: a wide neoprene belt designed to keep the body core warm

kneeboarders/kneelos: surfers who ride kneeling down

leash cup/plug: a fitting on the tail of the board where the surfer's leash is attached

left-breaking wave: a wave which breaks to the left when looking in toward the beach

neoprene wet suit: a suit made of a waterproof, stretchy rubber material

nose: the pointed front of the board

off the face: a maneuver off the face of the wave

off the lip: a maneuver off the breaking lip of the wave

off the top: a maneuver off the top of the wave

offset: fins set to one side in the tail, for riding a particular break

ollie-pop: a skateboard trick turned into a surfing aerial

plane: to skim across the water, with most of the board lifted clear of the surface

planing area: the small part of the tail which stays on the water when the board planes

point break: a break caused by a headland or promontory

promontory: a point of high land jutting out to sea

rails: the sides of the board

reentry: getting back on to the wave face

reef break: wave breaking on a reef

regular stance: standing with your left foot forward on the board

right-breaking wave: a wave which breaks to the right when looking in toward the beach

rip current: the current which allows the water from a broken wave to flow back out to sea

rocker line: the curve from nose to tail of a surfboard when viewed from the side

roller coaster: a surfing maneuver across the top of a wave

sandbank break: waves breaking on a sandbank

shore break: waves breaking on the shore

sneaker waves: a surprise set of bigger waves coming through

soup: frothy white water

surf leash: an elasticized line securing the tail of the surfboard to the surfer's ankle

surf reports: weather reports giving wave information

swell: the action of the waves

tail: the back of the board

tail slide: letting the tail slide across the wave

takeoff: catching the wave

thermal efficiency: the warmth of a wet suit

three-fin thruster: a short, wide-tailed board with three small fins for directional stability

thrusters: a small group of 2–4 fins

top turn: taking off the top of the wave

tube: where the wave bowls over and forms a hollow tube in front of the face

undertow: an underwater current released by breaking waves, flowing out to sea

volume: the amount of flotation in a board, determined by the size of the foam core

wave face: the front of the wave

wave ski: a surfboard/surf canoe hybrid

wax: rubbed on to the deck of a surfboard to give good nonslip properties

wax comb: a heavily waxed surface is kept in good condition with a metal wax comb

weighting: pushing down either rail and leaning back or forward to make the board turn where you want to go

white water: the broken water of a wave; sometimes also called "soup"

wind swell: swell or waves created by local winds

wipeout: falling off in big waves

Index

DATE			